HISTORY
·V·I·P·

EMMELINE
PANKHURST

BRILLIANT
BIOGRAPHIES
of the
DEAD FAMOUS

Kay Barnham

First published in Great Britain in 2015 by Wayland
Copyright © Wayland 2015
All rights reserved.
Editor: Annabel Stones
Illustration: Emmanuel Cerisier, Beehive Illustration
Designer: Rocket Design (East Anglia) Ltd
Proofreader: Rebecca Clunes

Dewey number: 324.6'23'092-dc23
ISBN: 978 0 7502 8850 7
10 9 8 7 6 5 4 3 2 1

Wayland

An imprint of Hachette Children's Group
Part of Hodder & Stoughton
Carmelite House
50 Victoria Embankment
London EC4Y 0DZ

An Hachette UK Company
www.hachette.co.uk
www.hachettechildrens.co.uk

Printed in China

Picture credits: Getty Images: p15 Topical Press Agency, p17 Heritage Images,
p18 Ullstein Bild, p23 Popperfoto, p25 Topical Press Agency, p26 Heritage Images;
IstockPhoto: p13 © Linda Steward; Mary Evans Picture Library: p8 (top);
Shutterstock: p7 Martin M303, p8 (bottom) Everett Historical, p11 Everett Historical,
p29 Neftali; CC Wikimedia Commons: p20 Johnny Cyprus.
All graphic elements courtesy of Shutterstock.

CONTENTS

page

Introducing EMMELINE PANKHURST ←→ 4

a DRAMATIC FAMILY ←→ 6

the BATCHELOR BARRISTER ←→ 8

VOTES FOR *all* WOMEN ←→ 10

STEPPING *into* POLITICS ←→ 12

WHAT EMMELINE DID NEXT ←→ 14

TAKING ACTION ←→ 16

PRISON! ←→ 18

ON THE MOVE ←→ 20

DEEDS *not* WORDS ←→ 22

WAR *and* PEACE ←→ 24

FIGHTING UNTIL THE END ←→ 26

THE VOTE, AT LAST ←→ 28

TIMELINE ←→ 30

GLOSSARY *and* FURTHER INFORMATION ←→ 31

INDEX ←→ 32

Introducing
EMMELINE PANKHURST

In the nineteenth century, very few people were allowed to vote in the UK – and they were all men. Henry VI had decided in 1432 that male landowners would be the only people allowed to vote. This law remained unchanged for four centuries. This meant that women, and many men, had no say in who was elected to run the country. One woman decided to change that!

WHO WAS SHE?

FULL NAME: *Emmeline Pankhurst (born Emmeline Goulden)*

DATE OF BIRTH: *15 July 1858*

LIVED: *Manchester and London, UK*

PARENTS: *Sophia Craine and Robert Goulden*

SIBLINGS: *10*

JOB: *Political activist*

MARRIED: *Richard P...*

CHILDREN: *Christabel, Francis Henry, ... Henry Francis*

DIED: *14 June 19...*

The law had changed in 1832 with the Representation of the People Act. This act allowed men who paid more than £10 a year to rent property to vote too. However, in those days £10 was a huge sum of money that only a few could afford to pay. Still, only one man in every seven could vote.

When Emmeline Pankhurst was born in 1858, not a single woman had the right to cast a vote in an election. She didn't think this was fair. She wanted it to be the law that all adults were allowed to vote in political elections.

TRUE or FALSE?

EMMELINE PANKHURST DIDN'T THINK THAT SHE WAS BORN ON 15 JULY AT ALL.

true She believed that her real birthday was actually 14 July – Bastille Day in France. The day commemorates the storming of the Bastille prison in Paris and the beginning of the French Revolution. She said, 'I have always thought that the fact that I was born on that day had some kind of influence over my life.'

WELL I NEVER!

The word 'suffrage' comes from the Latin word 'suffragium', which means the right to vote. It has nothing to do with suffering.

a DRAMATIC FAMILY

The Goulden family had often stood up for what they believed in. Emmeline's grandparents on her father's side took part in political unrest. Her mother was related to political activists on the Isle of Man, one of the first places to give women the vote.

Her father was involved in politics too. He was a town councillor in Manchester, where they lived. He also loved acting. Robert Goulden owned a theatre and starred in Shakespeare plays performed there.

★ Suffrage ★

The right to vote in political elections is known as suffrage. Those who fought for that right were known as suffragists. In the nineteenth century, women struggled to be treated the same way as men in many different ways. But it was the fight for voting rights that became their most important campaign.

Emmeline's parents strongly believed that women should be able to vote in elections. Her mother was a keen reader of the *Women's Suffrage Journal*. Soon, 14-year-old Emmeline was reading it too. When she discovered that the editor of the journal would be speaking at a public meeting, Emmeline was desperate to go with her mother. It would be the start of a lifetime spent supporting women's suffrage.

When she was 15, Emmeline went to a finishing school in Paris, where girls learned to behave, speak and walk like ladies. But at the *École Normale Supérieure*, girls were also taught subjects that were usually reserved for boys. So Emmeline studied science and maths too.

Emmeline studied in Paris when she was 15.

WELL I NEVER!

Emmeline took part in her first demonstration when she was just 10 years old! The feminist demonstration happened in the run-up to the 1868 General Election.

the BACHELOR BARRISTER

In 1878, Emmeline met a lawyer who was a big supporter of women's suffrage. Richard Pankhurst had devoted his life to political causes and had not planned to marry. He was 24 years older than Emmeline, and her mother did not approve of the match. But Emmeline was determined and they did get married, in 1879.

It was because of Richard Pankhurst that the law changed to allow married women to vote in local elections. He was also responsible for the law that meant when a woman married, she kept any property she already owned. It no longer automatically belonged to her husband.

Richard Pankhurst

Richard and Emmeline had five children. But just because they had a family didn't mean that Emmeline gave up doing what she believed in. They employed a nanny, so that Emmeline still had time to support women's suffrage.

IN OTHER NEWS

THOMAS EDISON

In 1879, American inventor Thomas Edison registered the idea for the light bulb. It glowed for 40 hours. But after much experimenting and many different versions, Edison's light bulb was improved so much that it glowed for 1500 hours!

In 1886, the Pankhurst family moved from Manchester to London, where Richard tried to become a Member of Parliament, or MP. Unfortunately, he didn't succeed. Then their son Francis died from a disease called diphtheria in 1888. The Pankhursts blamed the death on the poor area in which they lived and the family moved to a wealthier part of London soon afterwards. It was here, in Russell Square, that the Pankhursts began to receive important political visitors.

TRUE or FALSE?

EMMELINE DIDN'T ACTUALLY WANT TO GET MARRIED TO RICHARD.

true It was Richard who persuaded her that they should formally wed. In the nineteenth century, living together was frowned upon and he worried that Emmeline would be ignored by society if she didn't follow its rules.

VOTES FOR *all* WOMEN

At the end of the nineteenth century, a number of groups supported women's suffrage in the UK. But although they all wanted the vote for women, they disagreed about which women exactly they were fighting for. One group, called the Parliament Street Society, decided that it was easier fighting for just single women and widows to get the vote. The Pankhursts did not agree.

WELL I NEVER!

Emmeline Pankhurst was once a shopkeeper, selling home furnishings in London. But her shop was in one of the poorer areas of the city and the products were too grand and too expensive for local customers. Unfortunately, it soon closed.

The reason many thought that married women did not need to vote was because they assumed a wife's opinion would naturally be the same as her husband's. So his vote would count for both of them.

The Pankhursts thought that ALL women should be allowed to vote for what they believed in – married women included. So, in 1889, they helped create the Women's Franchise League (WFL) to fight for this. They didn't just want equal rights for women's votes. The WFL wanted women to have the same divorce and inheritance rights as men.

In 1890, the WFL broke up when members disagreed with each other. But it wasn't the end of Emmeline Pankhurst's fight.

★ **The Cause** ★

In the nineteenth century, women's fight for equality was known as The Cause. Even though the campaign for voting rights was only one of the areas in which women wanted the same rights as men, suffrage became the flagship of The Cause. Suffragists hoped that if women had the same voting rights as men, then other rights would follow.

Women all around the world campaigned for the right to vote. These suffragists are in the USA.

STEPPING into POLITICS

After the Women's Franchise League disbanded, Emmeline turned her attention to mainstream politics. Perhaps, if she joined a political party, this would be a way of promoting women's rights. Emmeline chose the Independent Labour Party (ILP). The first step was to join the party's local branch, but they turned her down – because she was a woman. Emmeline refused to give up and joined the ILP's national party instead.

By 1893, the Pankhursts were running out of money. Emmeline's father refused to help them and so she never spoke to him again. As most of Richard Pankhurst's clients were in Manchester, they decided to leave London and moved back to the north-west of England.

In Manchester, Emmeline really began to make a name for herself. She threw herself into the ILP's activities and began giving out food to the poor. When she was elected as a workhouse guardian, she saw for herself the terrible conditions in which the very poor were living.

TRUE or FALSE?

RICHARD PANKHURST WAS KNOWN AS THE BLUE DOCTOR.

false He was known as the Red Doctor, because he stood for parliament as an Independent Labour Party candidate in 1883 and the colour associated with the Labour Party is red.

In Victorian workhouses, the poor could work in return for food and a place to sleep.

WHAT SHE SAID

The first time I went into the place I was horrified to see little girls seven and eight years old on their knees scrubbing the cold stones of the long corridors ... bronchitis was epidemic among them most of the time ... I found that there were pregnant women in that workhouse, scrubbing floors, doing the hardest kind of work, almost until their babies came into the world ...

Emmeline Pankhurst, after visiting a workhouse in Manchester.

WHAT EMMELINE DID NEXT

In 1898, tragedy struck when Richard Pankhurst died. This came as a huge shock to Emmeline. She now had to look after her family on her own, as well as deal with the debt in which her husband's death had left them. Emmeline moved to a cheaper house and got a job as a registrar. This work revealed more and more about the terrible lives that some women led.

Emmeline began to see how laws often made life much more difficult for women than men. She now felt even more strongly that women needed the vote, so that their opinions could be heard.

Emmeline decided that political parties were unlikely to help her suffrage cause. They were campaigning about so many different things that votes for women didn't get enough publicity. When politicians did make promises and speeches about suffrage, nothing seemed to change. So she left the ILP and formed the Women's Social and Political Union – a women-only group. The WSPU would be dedicated to winning the vote for women.

The WSPU used different tactics to other political parties. They swapped polite meetings for noisy demonstrations. And they weren't afraid to break the law to get themselves and their ideas noticed.

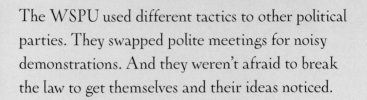

Emmeline Pankhurst (centre right) with her daughter, Christabel (left).

TRUE or FALSE?

NONE OF THE PANKHURSTS' DAUGHTERS WERE INVOLVED IN THE FIGHT FOR WOMEN'S VOTING RIGHTS.

false Christabel (1880–1958), Sylvia (1882–1960) and Adela (1885–1961) *all* became suffragettes. Christabel and Sylvia helped their mother to run the WSPU.

WHAT THEY SAID

'Deeds, not words.'

This was motto of the Women's Social and Political Union.

TAKING ACTION

The action that the WSPU took was designed to draw attention to themselves and the suffrage cause. They disrupted public meetings. They marched and went on demonstrations. They even used violence. When Christabel Pankhurst and another WSPU member heckled MP Winston Churchill at a meeting in 1905, the crowd was shocked. This wasn't how women usually behaved. When the women raised a banner that read 'VOTES FOR WOMEN', they were arrested.

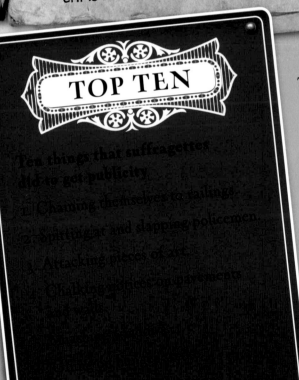

TOP TEN

Ten things that suffragettes did to get publicity

1. Chaining themselves to railings
2. Spitting at and slapping policemen
3. Attacking pieces of art
4. Chalking notices on pavements

This was just the start. When politicians prevented a law being passed for women's suffrage, the WSPU demonstrated outside the Houses of Parliament in London to show how unhappy they were. The suffragettes were pushed away by the police, but they came back, time and time again.

Soon, the protests turned violent and the police took action. The punishment for breaking the law was imprisonment. All three of Emmeline's daughters were sent to prison. Then, after a protest in 1908, Emmeline Pankhurst herself was arrested, charged and sentenced to six weeks in Holloway Prison.

A riot began when the suffragettes were refused permission to present a petition to the King.

WELL I NEVER!

The term 'suffragette' was first used by *Daily Mail* journalist Charles Hands in 1906 to describe WSPU members. Until then, all suffrage supporters had been known as suffragists.

PRISON!

Emmeline Pankhurst soon realised that even though prison was no fun at all, it did have one benefit. It was an excellent way of getting publicity for the fight for women's suffrage. So after her first six-week sentence in Holloway Prison in 1908, Emmeline broke the law again and again. Once, she even slapped a policeman, to make sure she'd be arrested.

In prison, a suffragette called Marion Wallace Dunlop came up with another way to keep the protest in the news. She went on hunger strike, refusing all food. She was released after a few days. Others did the same. But so many of the suffragettes went on hunger strike that the prison guards got tough. They force-fed the suffragettes to make sure they didn't starve.

Force-feeding was a violent way of making someone eat. A long rubber tube was inserted into the hunger-striking suffragette's mouth or nose, and then down their throat into their stomach. Liquid food was then poured into a funnel and down the tube. Many members of the public were horrified by this treatment.

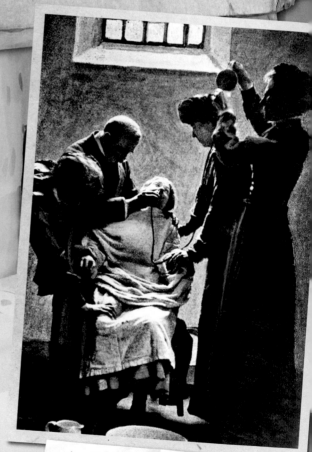

A suffragette is force-fed in prison.

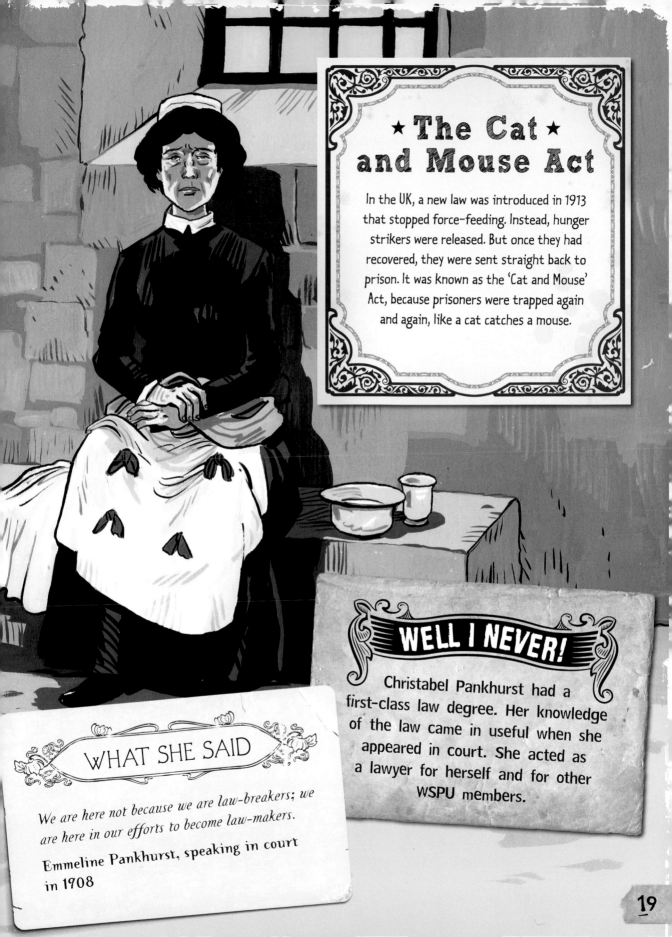

★ The Cat ★ and Mouse Act

In the UK, a new law was introduced in 1913 that stopped force-feeding. Instead, hunger strikers were released. But once they had recovered, they were sent straight back to prison. It was known as the 'Cat and Mouse' Act, because prisoners were trapped again and again, like a cat catches a mouse.

WELL I NEVER!

Christabel Pankhurst had a first-class law degree. Her knowledge of the law came in useful when she appeared in court. She acted as a lawyer for herself and for other WSPU members.

WHAT SHE SAID

We are here not because we are law-breakers; we are here in our efforts to become law-makers.

Emmeline Pankhurst, speaking in court in 1908

ON THE MOVE

Emmeline Pankhurst no longer had her own home. In 1907, she had sold her house in Manchester so that she could concentrate on the WSPU's work. Now she lived out of suitcases, staying with friends or at hotels. She was free to travel around and speak at rallies all over the country, to encourage others to support women's suffrage. Unfortunately, it also meant that she was often apart from her children.

TRUE or FALSE?

THE WSPU'S OFFICIAL COLOURS WERE RED, WHITE AND BLUE.

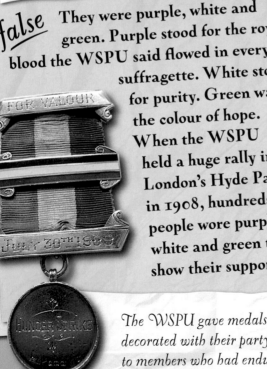

false They were purple, white and green. Purple stood for the royal blood the WSPU said flowed in every suffragette. White stood for purity. Green was the colour of hope. When the WSPU held a huge rally in London's Hyde Park in 1908, hundreds of people wore purple, white and green to show their support.

The WSPU gave medals decorated with their party colours to members who had endured the hardship of the hunger strike.

20

There was terrible news in 1909, when Harry Pankhurst was paralysed after a serious illness. Emmeline needed to earn money to pay for her son's treatment, so she still had to go on a tour of the US. The tour went well and she came back to care for her son, but Harry died the next year.

By 1910, the future was looking brighter for the suffragettes. A group of MPs from different parties got together to work on a bill that would give the vote to women who owned property. Even though the Prime Minister, Herbert Asquith, supported the bill, many MPs did not. Some did not want women to vote. Others wanted all women to vote. Some MPs worried that if women got the vote, they would elect another party – not theirs. The bill failed. So did further bills in 1911 and 1912.

WELL I NEVER!

The WSPU protested against any political party that did not support suffrage. After a Liberal candidate failed to win a seat at Parliament, his supporters blamed the WSPU and attacked them. The women were pelted with rotten eggs and snowballs with stones hidden inside them.

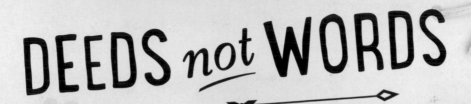

DEEDS not WORDS

By 1912, WSPU members were furious that after years of campaigning women still didn't have the vote. Their protests became more violent. It seemed they would stop at nothing to get publicity for women's votes. In fact, their activities became so daring that even their own members were shocked. Many left the WSPU in protest, including Emmeline's daughter, Adela.

WHAT SHE SAID

You have to make more noise than anybody else, you have to make yourself more obtrusive than anybody else, you have to fill all the papers more than anybody else, in fact you have to be there all the time and see that they do not snow you under, if you are really going to get your reform realised.

Emmeline Pankhurst

Suffragettes tried to blow up a Dublin theatre. They set fire to a café in a London park, postboxes and a railway carriage. They even smuggled a hatchet into the Prime Minister's carriage. Not all of these crimes were carried out by WSPU members, but Emmeline Pankhurst supported them anyway. However, many thought it unfair that the WSPU leaders made all the decisions, and that members were expected to just follow orders.

Then on 4 June 1913, suffragette Emily Wilding Davison ran in front of King George V's horse at the Epsom Derby. She may have been trying to attach a Votes for Women sash around the horse's neck. But she was trampled underneath its hooves and died four days later from her injuries. Her death hit the headlines and when she was buried, thousands came to pay their respects.

WHO WAS SHE?

NAME: Emily Wilding Davison
DATE OF BIRTH: 11 October 1872

Charles and Margaret

Two sisters, a brother half-sisters and half-

EDUCATION: She studied biology, chemistry, English language and literature at the University of Oxford. She was awarded first-class honours, but not a degree because at the time, degrees were just for men.

JOB: Teacher and suffragette
DIED: 8 June 1913

The
Suffragette
The Official Organ of the
Women's Social and Political Union
Edited by Christabel Pankhurst.
No. 35 — Vol. 1.   FRIDAY, JUNE 13, 1913.   Price 1d. Weekly

IN HONOUR AND IN LOVING, REVERENT MEMORY
OF
EMILY WILDING DAVISON.
SHE DIED FOR WOMEN.

This edition of 'The Suffragette' commemorated the death of Emily Wilding Davison.

WAR and PEACE

When World War One began, Emmeline and her daughter Christabel put a stop to all violent action. They decided it was time to support their government, not fight against it. The WSPU stopped campaigning for women's votes and focused instead on the war effort. But some suffrage groups were unhappy that the WSPU was working with the government. Meanwhile, Emmeline's other daughters – Sylvia and Adela – were not happy either. They were pacifists and campaigned against war.

Emmeline was now totally devoted to the war effort. She made speeches and encouraged women to work, doing the jobs that were left vacant while men were away fighting. She opened a home for the children of unmarried mothers and she adopted four herself. Then in 1916, she travelled to North America, to encourage the US to join the war. After four long years, World War One – in which millions had died – came to an end in 1918.

A month after the end of the war, something astonishing happened: parliament finally passed a bill that gave women the vote, though not all of them.

There are many theories as to why MPs changed their minds. Some say that women were being rewarded for their efforts during the war. Others say that MPs didn't want the suffragettes to start protesting again now the war was over. But whatever the reason, for the first time ever, some women could now vote.

WHAT SHE SAID

"[W]hen the time comes we shall renew that fight," she said, "but for the present we must all do our best to fight a common foe."

Emmeline Pankhurst

WELL I NEVER!

Emmeline and her daughter Sylvia disagreed over some of the WSPU's actions and Sylvia left the organisation. Then, disappointed in her youngest daughter, Adela, Emmeline told her to emigrate and paid for her to move to Australia.

★ The ★ Representation of the People Act 1918

This Act of Parliament allowed women over the age of 30 to vote, but only if they were a member of local government or were married to one, owned property or were a graduate voting at university. Meanwhile, all men aged 21 and over could now vote.

Emmeline addresses a crowd in New York, USA, in 1911.

25

FIGHTING UNTIL THE END

After the war, Emmeline Pankhurst carried on her struggle for equal rights for women. She wanted all women over 21 to get the vote, just like men. The WSPU became the Women's Party and many members wanted Emmeline to become an MP. As an MP, she could fight for women's rights in Parliament. Emmeline refused. She thought her daughter Christabel stood a much better chance of winning a seat in the 1918 election and supported her tirelessly. But Christabel lost by a few hundred votes.

WHAT SHE SAID

I come to ask you to help to win this fight. If we win it, this hardest of all fights, then ... in the future it is going to be made easier for women all over the world to win their fight when their time comes.

Excerpt from Pankhurst's Freedom or Death speech in Connecticut, USA, in 1913

From left: Emmeline, Christabel and Sylvia Pankhurst

Bitterly disappointed, Emmeline Pankhurst now focused on her country. She wanted to tell everyone how great the British Empire was and she travelled many times to North America to do just that. She was so impressed by women's rights in Canada that she actually moved there in 1922. But the long winters tired her and she moved back to the UK three years later.

In 1926, Emmeline Pankhurst began her last fight. She decided that she did want to become an MP after all. But even though she became a Conservative Party candidate in 1927, Emmeline never got the chance to take part in the 1929 general election. Weakened by her many, many hunger strikes, she died in 1928, aged 69.

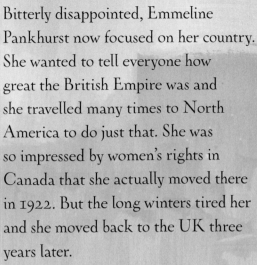

TRUE or FALSE?

TWO OF EMMELINE PANKHURST'S DAUGHTERS WROTE ABOUT HER. THEY BOTH HEAPED HER WITH PRAISE.

false Christabel wrote about how generous Emmeline Pankhurst was and how she would always help others. However, Sylvia criticised her mother.

THE VOTE, AT LAST

Emmeline Pankhurst died just two weeks before the UK government passed the Representation of the People Act 1928. The act gave all women over the age of 21 the vote, just like men. Finally, in 1969, the minimum voting age was dropped to 18 for all.

TRUE or FALSE?

PANKHURST FEATURES IN THE 1964 MUSICAL MARY POPPINS

true In the film, the character Mrs Banks, who is campaigning for votes for women, sings the song *Sister Suffragette*. The lyrics mention 'Mrs Pankhurst' and 'equal rights'.

Historians disagree on whether the WSPU's violent protests helped to win the fight for women's votes or turned public opinion against the suffragettes and made it more difficult. But there is no doubt that Emmeline Pankhurst and the WSPU kept the subject of women's votes in the news. And while it was in the news, it wasn't a subject that the government could ignore.

In 1929, a portrait of Emmeline Pankhurst was hung in the National Portrait Gallery in London. The following year, her statue was unveiled in Victoria Tower Gardens, near the Houses of Parliament. But perhaps the best way to remember Emmeline Pankhurst is the fact that in the twenty-first century, it is totally normal for women to vote.

POLLING STATION

1st

EMMELINE PANKHURST
NATIONAL PORTRAIT GALLERY

2006

In 2006, Emmeline Pankhurst was honoured when her portrait appeared on a postage stamp in the UK.

WELL I NEVER!

MOST IMPORTANT PEOPLE OF THE 20TH CENTURY

In 1999, *Time* magazine published a list of the most important people of the century. Only the top three people were ranked, but Pankhurst was one of the other 97 people listed.

1. Albert Einstein (1879–1955) Scientist

2. Franklin D Roosevelt (1882–1945) US president

3. Mahatma Gandhi (1869–1948) Politician and pacifist

Emmeline Pankhurst (1858–1928) Political activist

Time (1999)

BALLOT BOX

TIMELINE

1432   Henry VI decides that male landowners are the only people who can vote.

1858   Emmeline Goulden is born.

1868   She takes part in her first demonstration.

1879   Emmeline marries Richard Pankhurst.

1880   Christabel Pankhurst is born.

1882   Sylvia Pankhurst is born.

1885   Adela Pankhurst is born.

1889   The Pankhursts help create the Women's Franchise League.

1890   The Women's Franchise League breaks up.

1898   Richard Pankhurst dies.

1903   The Women's Social and Political Union (WSPU) is formed.

1905   Christabel Pankhurst is arrested and imprisoned.

1908   Emmeline Pankhurst is arrested and imprisoned.

1910   The WSPU holds a huge rally in Hyde Park, London.

1913   Emily Wilding Davison dies while protesting at Epsom Derby.

1914   World War One begins. Suffragettes are released from prison.

1918   World War One ends. Parliament passes a bill that gives some women the vote.

1928   Emmeline Pankhurst dies. Two weeks later, the vote is given to all women over the age of 21.

GLOSSARY

bachelor a man who has not been married

barrister a lawyer who appears in court

bill a law that is discussed by parliament

British Empire a group of countries that used to be ruled by Britain

campaign an organised way of trying to change something

candidate someone who nominated for a position

cause an idea that people work together to support

demonstration many people meeting or marching together to show their views on a political issue

election an event where people vote for who will run their country

epidemic when many, many people have the same disease

feminist someone who believes that women should have the same rights as men

MP Member of Parliament; a person who represents a group of people in the UK government

obtrusive something that is noticeable or stands out

pacifist someone who believes that arguments should be settled peacefully

parliament the group of people who decide the laws in a country

politics the work of government

publicity a way of letting everyone know about something

reform when things are changed

registrar someone who keeps official records

suffrage the right to vote

suffragette a woman trying to win the right to vote, by protest

suffragist someone who thinks that more people should be able to vote, especially women

unrest a time when many people are unhappy about a political issue, usually involving demonstrations

vote to say which candidate or idea should be chosen

workhouse a place where very poor people could eat and sleep in return for hard work

further information

BOOKS

Opal Plumstead by Jacqueline Wilson (Corgi Children's, 2015)

Suffragette (My Story) by Carol Drinkwater (Scholastic, 2011)

Suffragette: My Own Story by Emmeline Pankhurst (Hesperus Classics, 2015)

WEBSITES

www.bbc.co.uk/bitesize/higher/history/britsuff/suffrage/revision/1/
BBC history of the women's suffrage movement.

www.theschoolrun.com/homework-help/the-suffragettes
Information, a timeline, facts, photos, games and much more about the suffragettes.

PLACES TO VISIT

The Pankhurst Centre,
60–62 Nelson Street, Manchester, M13 9WP

National Portrait Gallery,
St Martin's Place, London WC2H 0HE

Victoria Tower Gardens, London, SW1P 3JA

INDEX

A
adoption 24
Asquith, Herbert 21

B
birthday 5

C
Canada 27
'Cat and Mouse' Act 19
Cause, The 11
Churchill, Winston 16
Conservative Party 27

D
Davison, Emily Wilding 23
demonstrations 7, 15, 16
diphtheria 9
Dunlop, Marion Wallace 18

E
Edison, Thomas 8
Epsom Derby 23

F
force-feeding 18, 19

G
George V 23
Goulden family (Emmeline's parents) 4, 6, 7, 8, 12

H
Henry VI 4
hunger strikes 16, 18, 19, 20, 27

I
Independent Labour Party (ILP) 12, 14

L
landowners 4, 25 *see also* property
lawyer 8, 19
London 4, 9, 10, 12, 16, 20, 23, 28

M
Manchester 4, 6, 9, 12, 13, 20
marriage 8, 9, 11, 24, 25
Mary Poppins 28
medals 20
Member of Parliament (MP) 9, 16, 21, 24, 26, 27
motto 15

N
National Portrait Gallery 28

P
pacifist 24, 29
Pankhurst, Adela 4, 15, 22, 24, 25
Pankhurst, Christabel 4, 15, 16, 19, 24, 26, 27
Pankhurst, Francis 4, 9
Pankhurst, Henry 4, 21
Pankhurst, Richard 4, 8, 9, 12, 14
Pankhurst, Sylvia 4, 15, 24, 25, 26, 27
Paris 5, 7
Parliament Street Society 10
police 16, 17, 18
prison 5, 17, 18-19
property 5, 8, 21, 25

R
rallies 20
Red Doctor 12
registrar 14
Representation of the People Act
1832 5
1918 24, 25
1928 28

S
school 7

T
'The Suffragette' magazine 23
Time magazine 29

U
USA 11, 24, 25, 26, 27

W
Women's Franchise League (WFL) 11, 12
Women's Party 26
Women's Social and Political Union (WSPU) 14, 15, 16, 19, 20, 21, 22, 23, 26, 28
colours 20
Women's Suffrage Journal 7
workhouse 12, 13
World War One 24, 31

More history titles available
from Wayland...

Best and Worst Jobs in...

978 0 7502 8736 4

978 0 7502 8740 1

Truth or Busted

978 0 7502 8129 4

978 0 7502 8130 0

What they don't tell you about...

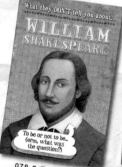

978 0 7502 8167 6

978 0 7502 8047 1

Awfully Ancient

978 0 7502 7991 8

978 0 7502 7987 1

EPIC

978 0 7502 8761 6

978 0 7502 8755 5

Explore!

978 0 7502 8860 6

978 0 7502 9549 9